Refle

Dietrich Bonhoeffer

Reflections on the Bible

Human Word and Word of God

Edited by Manfred Weber

Translated by M. Eugene Boring

P. O. Box 3473
Peabody, Massachusetts 01961-3473

ISBN 1-56563-988-X

Translated from Dietrich Bonhoeffer, *Die Antwort auf unsere Fragen: Gedanken zur Bibel*, edited by Manfred Weber, © 2002, Gütersloher Verlagshaus GmbH, Gütersloh, Germany.

Printed in the United States of America

First Printing—September 2004

Library of Congress Cataloging-in-Publication Data

Bonhoeffer, Dietrich, 1906–1945.
[Antwort auf unsere Fragen. English]
Reflections on the Bible : human word and Word of God / Dietrich Bonhoeffer ; edited by Manfred Weber ; translated by M. Eugene Boring.
p. cm.
Includes bibliographical references.
ISBN 1-56563-988-X (alk. paper)
1. Bible—Theology. 2. Word of God (Theology) I. Weber, Manfred. II. Title.
BS543.B58 2004
220.6—dc22

2004014505

Contents

"I believe that the Bible alone is the answer to all our questions and that to receive an answer from it, we only need to ask with persistence and a little courage."

Dietrich Bonhoeffer
DBW 14, 144–45

Introduction

"At the time of his confirmation he had already become an independent reader of the Bible, and there was no novel to be found between its black covers."[1]

This biographical note by Eberhard Bethge is not unimportant in understanding what it meant for Dietrich Bonhoeffer to read the Bible, or to "come to the Bible for the first time," as he once expressed it in a letter (see p. 9).

Bonhoeffer called the Bible "Holy Scripture" and "word of God." In selecting the texts for this book, the determining factor has been that his statements about the Bible and his own struggle with these statements—conceived, spoken, and written in a different time—show themselves to be extraordinarily up-to-date, for individuals and for the churches, for Christians and non-Christians.

In the 2002 Easter edition of a national newspaper we read, "The Bible is a book without which one understands nothing." The reference here is not to biblical history but to the events of our own time. "It would be senseless to try to conceal that the Bible is a book of faith. But this does not mean it is only a book for believers. Again and again it has been the case that the Bible ignites not faith but doubt."[2] This is the situation in which Bonhoeffer's texts open themselves to us, challenging and helping at the same time.

The texts are of differing genres: letters, meditations, expositions, sermons, lectures, seminar papers. This variety presents us with a spectrum of approaches to the subject matter, some easier than others, but taken together they make clear what a central role the Bible plays and how important it is for academic study, sermons, teaching, pastoral care, and the conduct of one's personal life.

The topics addressed in this book stretch from thematic study of the historical-critical method to a study of selected portions of Psalm 119. In the winter of 1939–1940, Bonhoeffer intensified his years-long engagement with this psalm and came to regard an interpretation of Psalm 119 "as the crown of a theological life."[3]

The texts are arranged according to the data of Bonhoeffer's own life. The two exceptions are the insertions into the chapters "Human Word and Word of God" and "Old Testament and New Testament," made for reasons of content. The collection is intentionally framed with the selections at the beginning and the end, "A Grand Liberation" and "The Answer." Both texts come from letters from the year 1936 and provide helpful approaches to the theme of this book. The first letter points "in very personal words to the revolutionary turn in the life of this productive theologian through his encounter with the Bible."[4] The second letter is a pastoral letter to an educated, involved, but somewhat aloof layman, explaining "what it actually means to confess faith in the Bible, the strange place where the strange word of God is heard. Engagement with the Bible involves an intensive seeking and questioning. Without this, the Bible will offer no answer."[5]

The texts in between are not arranged according to some systematic scheme but are intended to point, in an almost exaggerated manner, to Bonhoeffer's struggle with the Bible. His own spelling, orthography, and punctuation have been retained.

Dietrich Bonhoeffer sought, in and with the Bible, to find answers to the questions with which Christianity, and thus the churches, should be engaged. He sought an answer to the question why for us human beings there is "only one kind of life worth living" (see p. 107).[6] In a challenge and warning from a theologian of our own time, a fundamental concern of Dietrich Bonhoeffer's meets us anew: "Instead of incessantly tinkering with reformulating and transmitting its own words, the church should cultivate a school of hearing, a school oriented to hearing the Bible and hearing our fellow human beings."[7]

What is valid for the church applies to the individual. And for the individual there remains "the decision whether we are willing to trust the word of the Bible or not" (see p. 112).

Easter 2002 *Manfred Weber*

Notes to Introduction

1. DB 61. The reference is to evasion of a family rule. The children were not supposed to read in bed after the specified "lights out" time. Reading the Bible was the only exception acknowledged by the children's nanny. Dietrich's older brother Klaus evaded the rule by concealing an exciting novel inside the black covers of a Bible. [Translator]

2. Jan Ross, "Faust, Freud, Bach, und die Bible," *Die Zeit* (March 27, 2002).

3. DB 750.

4. DBW 14:999.

5. DBW 14:999.

6. DBW 14:144.

7. Friedrich-Wilhelm Marquardt, "Zuhören, weniger reden!" *Süddeutsche Zeitung* (March 13, 2002).

The death of his brother Walther and the unmanageable pain of their mother made an indelible impression on the child Dietrich Bonhoeffer. At his confirmation three years later, she presented to him the Bible that Walther had received in 1914 at his own confirmation. For the rest of his life, Bonhoeffer used it in his personal devotions and in worship.

Walther Bonhoeffer was wounded on April 23, 1918, and died on April 28, 1918.

A Grand Liberation

I threw myself into the work in a very unchristian and rather arrogant manner. A mind-boggling ambition, which many have noticed about me, made my life difficult and separated me from the love and trust of my fellow human beings. At that time I was terribly alone and left to my own devices. That was really a terrible time. Then something different happened, something that has changed my life, turned it around to this very day. I came to the Bible for the first time. It is terribly difficult for me to say that. I had already preached several times, had seen a lot of the church, had given speeches about it and written about it—but I had still not become a Christian, I was very much an untamed child, my own master. I know, at that time I had turned this whole business about Jesus Christ into an advantage for myself, a kind of crazy vanity. I pray God, it will never be so again. I had also never prayed, or at least not much and not really. With all my loneliness, I was still quite pleased with myself. It was from this that the Bible—especially the Sermon on the Mount—freed me. Since then everything is different. I am clearly aware of it myself; and even those around me have noticed it. That was a grand liberation. There it became clear to me that the life of a servant of Jesus Christ must belong to the church, and gradually it became clearer how far this has to go. Then came the troubles of 1933. They only strengthened me in this. At this time I also found people who looked with me toward the same goal. I now saw that everything depended on the renewal of the church and of the ministry. . . . Christian pacifism, which I had previously fought against with passion, all at once seemed perfectly obvious. And so it went further, step by step. I saw and thought of nothing else. . . .

The authority of the Bible is not a thing that can be proved, but is determined by the faith decision of the individual or community.

Summer semester, 1932

Human Word and Word of God

The Christian religion stands and falls by its faith in divine revelation in history, a revelation that is real, tangible, visible—to those who have eyes to see and ears to hear. The Christian faith thus bears in its innermost core the question of the relation of history and spirit, or, in biblical terms, letter and Spirit, Scripture and revelation, human word and word of God. No one can be prohibited from regarding the Bible as one book among others; indeed we all must do this, for those who wrote it were human beings like everyone else. It is in fact exclusively with these presuppositions that the historian approaches the Bible, this one book among others, which of course has attained much more historical significance than the rest. For almost two thousand years, a historical approach to the Christian religion has rested on this foundation, that the Bible is of exceptional historical importance but is nonetheless one book among others. It is no wonder that historical criticism found here its first and abiding object of investigation, that here it learned to sharpen its weapons in the most refined manner.

Its general principles are based on the mechanistic picture of the universe taken over from the natural sciences, and its methods of investigation are primarily those of the natural sciences; any obligation to theology is switched off from the outset. This is the bedrock on which all historical investigation rests, and must do so. In order to be "universally valid," its knowledge must be established by the fundamental separation of the knowing subject and the object to be known; it must be understandable by every reasonable human being. The increasing interest in psychology, which brought with it new theories about how extraordinary psychological states can be understood, could not produce any decisive change in understanding the Bible—though incidentally, in relation to the mechanistic methods, they were an enormous step forward for historical knowledge as such. As illustrated by the form of the Bible, this procedure means that the concept of the canon must be rejected as meaningless. Text criticism and source analysis are applied, sources are identified, form criticism and history-of-religions approaches fragment the text into its smallest units. After thoroughly reducing the text to rubble, the critics depart from the battlefield, leaving behind debris and shavings, their work apparently done. In terms of its content, the biblical picture is smoothed out to correspond to the spirit of its time, miracle stories are paralleled, and yes, even the person of Jesus himself is stripped not only of his divine but of his human splendor and disappears without any distinguishing marks into the lists of rabbis, sages, and religious enthusiasts. Of course, the reflective historian will also recognize that this book deals with particularly strange and profound things, that one catches sight of figures of outstanding magnitude, and so forth—otherwise he would surely be a poor historian. But he would be no better a historian if he believed that with such observations he could show that the Bible is the word of God.

There is no historical access to the person of Jesus that would be obligatory for faith. Access to the historical Jesus must come by way of the Resurrected One, by way of the word of the resurrected Christ, who testifies to himself. It is the Risen One who himself creates faith and opens up access to historicity. From this point of view, the historian's word, whether it claims to affirm or deny Christ, is irrelevant. In faith, history is seen to be what it actually is from the point of view of eternity, not in terms of itself, from within.

At the same time it must be maintained that the testimony of Jesus as the Risen One is nothing else than what is presented to us by the Bible. We remain also clear-headed and objective as believers. We must read this book of books with all human methods. But through the fragile and broken Bible, God meets us in the voice of the Risen One.

And now if some among us must honestly say, "We haven't heard anything much," and others perhaps just as honestly believe they must say, "We have heard an enormous amount"—please permit me to express to both groups a deep concern that has increasingly burdened me during the whole conference: has it not again and again become terribly clear in all that we have said here to each other that we are no longer obedient to the Bible? We prefer our own ideas to those of the Bible. We no longer read the Bible seriously, no longer read it as against us but only as for us. If this whole conference is to have any real meaning, then it is perhaps this, that it shows us that before we meet again, we will have to learn to read the Bible in an entirely different way.

Dietrich Bonhoeffer in an address to the International Youth Congress in Gland, August 29, 1932

The Beginning

In the beginning God created the heavens and the earth. The earth was without form and void, and darkness was upon the face of the deep; and the Spirit of God was moving over the face of the waters.

Genesis 1:1–2 (RSV)

At the place on which the most passionate waves of our thinking break, are turned back on themselves, and dissipate—this is the place where the Bible begins. Its first word hardly becomes visible for an instant before the waves rage up again and the whitecaps cover it in foam. That the Bible presumes of the beginning at all is an irritation to the world, as it is to us. For we cannot speak of the beginning; where the beginning begins, our thought stops, comes to an end. And yet the innermost passion of our thinking, that which finally gives validity to every authentic question we ask, is that we want to ask about the beginning. We know that we always must ask the question of the beginning and yet can never ask this question. And why not? Because the Beginning is the Infinite and because we can think of the Infinite only as that which is without end and therefore precisely as that which is also without beginning. Because the beginning is freedom and it is always the case that we can only think of freedom in terms of necessity, as one thing among others, but never simply as the One before all others. If we ask why this is so, that we always think from the beginning and in reference to it and yet never have a conception of it, that we cannot even approach it by asking for or about it, this "Why?" still only points to a series that fades out into an endless regression and still never reaches the Beginning. Thinking can never answer its own ultimate "Why?" because each answer only generates a new "Why?"

We are presented with a double question: is this beginning God's beginning, or is it the beginning of God with the world? But even to raise this question already shows that we no longer know what "beginning" means. If "beginning" can only be talked about by those who are anxiously in the middle of things and wonder about beginning and end, by those who tear at their own chains, by those who know only from within their sinful situation that they are creatures of God—then it can no longer be asked whether this beginning is God's own beginning or God's beginning with the world. This is so because, for us, God as the beginning is simply no other than the One who at the beginning created the world and us and because we can know nothing at all of this God beyond the One who is the Creator of our world. When Luther was once asked what God had been doing before the creation of the world, he answered that God had been cutting switches for people who ask such useless questions. Luther thereby not only took the question away from the questioner but said at the same time that where God is not known as the gracious Creator, he must be known as the wrathful judge, that is, always in relation to the human situation in the middle of things, between beginning and end. There is no possible question that can get behind this God who stands at the beginning as the Creator. Nor can there be any question about the "why" of creation, about God's plan for bringing the world into being, about the necessity of creation—precisely these questions are done away with for good and exposed as godless questions by the sentence "In the beginning God created the heavens and the earth." Not that in the beginning God had this or that idea about the purpose of the world, thoughts that we might now trace out further, but that "in the beginning God *created*," and no question can get behind this creating God, because one cannot get back before the beginning.

It was "in the beginning" that God created heaven and earth, and that means in God's own freedom, out of nothing. This is the reassurance with which the Bible addresses us who live our lives in the middle of things, who anxiously stand before the false nothingness, the beginningless beginning and the endless end. It is the gospel, it is Christ, the Risen One himself, who is here spoken of. That God was at the beginning and will be there at the end, that he is free Lord of the world and that he lets us know that which is mercy, grace, forgiveness, reassurance.

The Word

Then God said,
'Let there be light'; and there was light.
Genesis 1:3

In distinction from all those creation myths in which the deity sacrifices its own nature, in which the world originates from the god's natural fertility, and thus in which the creation is understood as a kind of self-development or self-unfolding of the deity in which the deity "gives birth" to the universe so that the creation itself is part and parcel of the divine nature, so that nature's own suffering, its birth and passing away, is the suffering of the deity itself—in contrast to all this, the God of the Bible remains wholly God, wholly Creator, wholly the Lord, and his creation remains wholly the subordinate, obedient creation that responds to God in praise and prayer. God is never the creation; God is always the Creator. God is not the essence of nature; there is no continuum that would bind him and his creation together as one reality. There is only his *word.* God spoke . . . ; the only continuity between God and his work is the word. This means that "in itself" there is no continuum there. Without the word, the world plunges into the bottomless abyss. This word of God is not his nature, nor his essence, but his command—God himself is the One who by this word thinks and creates, but precisely as the One who wants to encounter the creation as its Creator. God's being as Creator is not a matter of God's nature or essence but God's will, God's command, in which God gives himself to us as he wills. That God creates by the word means that the creation is the command and behest of God and that this command is free. God *speaks,* which means he creates totally free from constraint and in his creative work remains entirely free in relation to his creation. God is not bound to his work, but he binds his work to himself. He does not unite himself with his work in terms of substance; rather, his relation to his work is his command, that is, he is never in the world in any other way than as absolutely transcending the world. God is *in* the world as his word, because he is the absolutely Transcendent One, and he is the absolutely Transcendent One because he is in the world *in his word.* Only in the word of creation do we know the Creator, only in the word in the midst of things do we have the beginning. Thus we do not recognize the Creator "from" his works, as though the substance, nature, essence of the work would now finally after all be somehow identical with God's nature, as though there were some kind of continuum, perhaps as represented by cause and effect; but only because God by his word acknowledges these works as his and because we *believe* these words about these works, we believe in God as the Creator.

That God *speaks* is first of all to be understood in the full sense of the word. "Word" means "spoken word," not "symbol," "meaning," "idea" but the thing designated by "word" itself. That God creates by speaking means that idea, name, and work are one in the created reality in God. Here everything depends on seeing that the meaning is not that the word has "effects" but that God's word *is* already a work. That which for us breaks hopelessly in two is for God inseparably one: the word of command and the event itself. For God, the imperative is already the indicative. The latter is not the result of the former but *is* it. So too, God's creative act cannot be described as "effective," as having an "effect," because such expressions lack the character of a command, the absolute freedom in creating that comes to expression in the word, that encompasses a definite reality, the freedom of the Creator from the creature. That it is done out of freedom is expressed by the "word," that it is done from authority is shown by the event. That it is absolutely impossible for us to think indicative and imperative together as one reality points to the reality that we no longer live in the unity of God's word that *is* a deed but live a fallen existence in a fallen world. For us, the connection between imperative and indicative can be thought of always only as a continuum, mostly within the framework of the cause-and-effect schema. This is what justifies us in inferring a "cause" from an "effect." But precisely this is what is not valid for thinking about the creation; it is not an "effect" of the Creator, from which one can read off a necessary connection with the "cause" (the Creator), but is a work created in freedom in the word.

Strangely enough, the Bible first says that God speaks, and, in speaking, creates, in connection with the creation of form, where God powerfully calls form to emerge from formlessness. Form corresponds to the word. The word calls forth, defines, the individual, the real, the whole. The word calls being out of nonbeing that it may be. It is an absolutely dark, completely inaccessible backdrop that emerges as the background for the creative word. It continues to be simply impossible for us to grasp that first wordless act of the creation, for the Creator is one, and as his creatures we are created by his word. These two moments are in God one act, and we cannot say it any other way.

"Let there be light"; and there was light. Because darkness prevailed over the formless deep, the light must create form. As the formless night receives form by the light of morning, as the light creates and unveils form, so the primeval light had to order the chaos, to create and unveil form. If this word about the darkness that prevailed on the deep was the first reference to the passion of Jesus Christ, so now the liberation of the subjected formless deep to be what it truly is through the light is a reference to the light that shines in the darkness. The light awakens the darkness to its own being, to the free praise of the Creator. Without the light we would not be, for without the light there is no over-againstness, because there is no form. But without the sense of being over against, there is no free worship of God. The subjected deep praises God

in its subjected, dull, imprisoned state of not being able to distinguish itself from the Other. In the light, form perceives this being-over-against as its own true being and gives thanks for this to the Creator alone. The transparency, clarity, and unburdened nature of its own being conferred by the light, aware of itself in its being distinct from other created forms and from the Creator, is the work of the first word of the Creator. In the light created by this word, the creation sees God's light.

Things are still going well with me, I am healthy, can go outside a half hour every day, and since I'm now allowed to smoke, I sometimes even forget briefly where I am! I am treated well, read a lot, besides the newspaper and novels, above all the Bible.

Dietrich Bonhoeffer to his parents,
Tegel prison, Easter Sunday, April 25, 1943

Unity

The Bible is the word of God, and a religious poem by Nietzsche is not. This is the unsolvable mystery of the revelation of God in hiddenness. It is really the biblical text as such that binds the whole Christian community into a unity. It assures us of our being bound together in one family of brothers and sisters not only with the Christian community of all past and future ages but with the whole church of the present. As such, the biblical text is of enormous unifying, ecumenical significance. This is to be understood not only as an objective reality (unity) but psychologically (unanimity). This consciousness of being bound together into one family is clearly strengthened among hearers of the biblical text, since this is an awareness that every deep insight and experience they encounter in this text is the agelong substance of Christian thought and life and so is heard and learned with gratitude and profound awe.

The End Time

Is it really through the cross and only through the cross that Christ goes to life, to resurrection, to victory? This is the startling theme of the Bible, which many find so repulsive, the premise that the only visible sign of God's presence in the world is the cross. Christ was not suddenly snatched up to heaven in clouds of glory but had to be raised up on the cross. And precisely there, where the cross stands, is the resurrection near. Precisely there, where all begin to have their doubts about God, where all despair of God's power, that is the place where God is really present, there the living Christ is near. At the place where one stands on the razor edge of decision, whether to become a deserter or to remain faithful—there is God, there is Christ totally. There, where the power of darkness wants to extinguish the light of God, there God triumphs and judges the darkness. So is it now, as Christ ponders the day that his church must face. His disciples ask him about the sign of his return after his death. This is not a return that happens only once but a return that is always happening. In the Bible, the end time is the whole time and every day between the death of Christ and the Last Judgment. Yes, this is how serious, how crucial, the New Testament sees the death of Christ.

The Gift of Truth

We have become accustomed to seeing religion as something that corresponds to a need of the human psyche, something that then satisfies this need. Something that is supposed to lead from the restlessness of our existence to calm, from the mad rush of our lives to tranquillity. Something in which, quite removed from our jobs, professions, and everyday lives, we can come to our true selves. Then we say religion is something beautiful, something valuable, something necessary for a good life. It is supposed to be the only thing that can make one truly happy in the depths of one's being.

Meanwhile we tend to forget the one decisive question, whether religion is also something true, whether it is the truth. For it could be, of course, that while religion is a beautiful thing, it is not true, that it is all a nice, pious illusion—but still an illusion. And the most furious attacks on religion have been sparked by the fact that people in the church itself have often talked as though the question of truth were only a secondary question. But whoever so speaks only sees religion from the perspective of human beings and their needs, not from that of God and his claims. This is why it is important for this one thing to become clear and that we allow it to be said to us from the New Testament: essentially only one thing matters about religion, namely, that it is true. Truth—this is the highest value not only in science but much more so and much more urgently in religion, which we want to make the foundation for our lives.

But how do I recognize that the subject matter of the Christian message is the truth? Here the Bible gives a strange answer: "Then Jesus said to the Jews who had believed in him, 'If you continue in my word, you are truly my disciples; and you will know the truth, and the truth will make you free' " (John 8:31–32). Not by unhindered and unbiased research, not by disinterested reflection and the search for truth, but only by freely testing it out in one's life, basing one's life entirely on the word of Christ, to live with him and by his example, to hear and obey him. Only the one who has staked his or her life on Christ as the truth is in a position to judge whether Christ speaks and is the truth. And Christ makes the promise: the one who dares to do this is the one who will recognize the truth. Truth is recognized only in the course of living it.

And finally: the truth will make you free! This is the gift of truth. The person who is upheld and sustained by the power of truth is the freest of all—afraid of nothing, bound by nothing. No prejudgment, no weak backing off when faced by deceitful hopes, but bound to one thing, the One, the Truth that is the truth of God that confers validity on all other truth. Whoever abides in the truth of God is truly free. God, make us free.

It is neither reasonable nor right—though one often hears it nowadays—to preach to a Christian congregation today that everyone must first become like Mary Magdalene, like poor Lazarus, like the thief on the cross, like one of the "marginalized figures" in the Bible, before one can hear the final word of God. However much one would like in this manner to emphasize the ultimacy of the word of God, what one in fact does is undermine it. The content of the Christian message is not that we should become like one of the minor biblical characters but to be—like Christ himself. There is no method that can make this happen; faith alone makes it possible. Otherwise the gospel is underrated, loses its value. Costly grace becomes cheap.

"Ultimate and Penultimate Things"
1940/1941

The Good News

There was a rich man who was dressed in purple and fine linen and who feasted sumptuously every day. And at his gate lay a poor man named Lazarus, covered with sores, who longed to satisfy his hunger with what fell from the rich man's table; even the dogs would come and lick his sores. The poor man died and was carried away by the angels to be with Abraham. The rich man also died and was buried. In Hades, where he was being tormented, he looked up and saw Abraham far away with Lazarus by his side. He called out, "Father Abraham, have mercy on me, and send Lazarus to dip the tip of his finger in water and cool my tongue; for I am in agony in these flames." But Abraham said, "Child, remember that during your lifetime you received your good things, and Lazarus in like manner evil things; but now he is comforted here, and you are in agony. Besides all this, between you and us a great chasm has been fixed, so that those who might want to pass from here to you cannot do

so, and no one can cross from there to us." He said, "Then, father, I beg you to send him to my father's house—for I have five brothers—that he may warn them, so that they will not also come into this place of torment." Abraham replied, "They have Moses and the prophets; they should listen to them." He said, "No, father Abraham; but if someone goes to them from the dead, they will repent." He said to him, "If they do not listen to Moses and the prophets, neither will they be convinced even if someone rises from the dead."

Luke 16:19–31

One cannot understand and proclaim the gospel concretely enough. When the gospel is rightly preached, it is as though one holds out a beautiful red apple to a child, or a glass of cold water to a person dying of thirst, and asks, "Do you want this?" To preach like this, we would have to be able to speak about the realities of our faith in the same way that our hands sometimes reach for something more quickly than we can control them. When the gospel is proclaimed, people must pursue it without rest, as sick people once pursued Christ the healer and savior as he journeyed about (though Christ himself healed more people than he converted). This is not just preacherly platitudes. Should it not really be this way wherever the good news of God is proclaimed? But as we all know—it is not this way.

We cannot reassure ourselves by claiming that it has to be that way. It is rather the case that we must always face up to the question why it is that way. And here is one—indeed, only one—of the reasons that we shy away from taking the gospel as concrete and realistic as it in fact is. We have spiritualized the gospel, which means we have changed it, made it easier than it is. Just take one example, the gospel reading about the rich man and poor Lazarus. It has become customary to see its whole meaning reduced to the principle that the rich should help the poor. That is, we take it as a moralizing example story. Yet precisely this story is something quite different from its usual interpretation if just once we let it have its original effect. It is not a lesson or example but a clear announcement of the good news itself—indeed, so plain, so severe, that we no longer take it seriously.

Just imagine a mass of sick, poor, suffering Lazaruses gathered around Christ. He began to tell of poor leprous Lazarus lying at the doorstep of the rich man, harassed even by the dogs. When the story came to the point where Jesus said, "The poor man died and was carried by the angels to be with Abraham. . . . 'Lazarus received evil during his life, but now he is comforted,' " shouts of joy and hope must have erupted in the group. That was the good news, that was the fresh water, for which they longed and reached out desperately. It was the love of God itself that spoke to the poor and suffering. You rejected, you disadvantaged, you poor and sick, you who are looked down upon—you will be comforted. You have endured much suffering in this world, but soon you will be engulfed in eternal joy and everlasting consolation. Look at poor Lazarus, how he lies disdained at the rich man's door, and then look at him, how he receives God's comfort in Abraham's bosom. "Blessed are you who are poor, for yours is the kingdom of God. Blessed are you who are hungry now, for you will be filled. Blessed are you who weep now, for you will laugh" (Luke 6:20–23). This is the way the Beatitudes are given in Luke. Here nothing is said about the "poor in spirit" (Matthew 5:3) or "hunger and thirst for righteousness" (Matthew 5:6), but "blessed are you poor, you hungry, you who cry," as we know you to be in this world. Blessed are you Lazaruses of all times, for you will be comforted in Abraham's bosom. Blessed are you rejected and disdained, you victims of society, you jobless men and women, you crushed and ruined, you abandoned and forsaken who have suffered violence, rape, and abuse, you miserable in body and soul. Blessed are you, for God's joy will come over you and rest on you forever. This is the gospel, the good news of the new world that is breaking in, the new order of things that is God's world and God's order. The deaf hear, the blind see, the lame walk, and good news is preached to the poor (Luke 7:22).

But before we interrupt ourselves with a few questions of our own, let's hear the other side of the story, the dreadful side. There is the rich man, clothed in purple and expensive linen. Here is what is said about him: "The rich man died and was buried." That already sounds a bit stern. And then in hell he must endure the pain of eternal thirst because on earth he has been full and satisfied. He has to see poor Lazarus in Abraham's bosom and beg that he could be sent to relieve his thirst for just one minute. But even this cannot happen. "But Abraham said, 'Child, remember that during your lifetime you received your good things.' " And in the background, we hear the words "Woe to you who are full now, for you will be hungry. Woe to you who are laughing now, for you will mourn and weep." Woe to you, who clothe yourselves in purple and live happily in a grand style, for you will have eternal thirst.

Blessed are you, poor leprous Lazarus of yesterday and today, for you have a God. Woe to you who live happily in a grand style, respected by others, yesterday and today. This is the concrete, plainly preached message of God's good news for the poor.

But before we continue, we must endure a series of indignant responses. There are always people in our midst who know what the New Testament can say and what it cannot say, and know this better than the New Testament itself. "What we have here," it is objected, "is a rough-and-ready interpretation of the New Testament, adapted for unsophisticated folk. There are in fact New Testament texts that sound like what we have said here, but what we need to do is interpret them in a more spiritual sense. We call this 'sublimation,' that is, a refinement, a raising of the text to another level, a spiritualizing, a moralizing. After all, it is not simply the objectively poor who are blessed and the objectively rich who are damned. The main thing is always how one relates to one's poverty or one's wealth. It is not primarily a matter of externals but of attitude: rich in regard to God, or poor in regard to God. . . ." The dangerous thing about this objection is that it does in fact contain some truth but still basically aims only at excusing ourselves. It is so terribly easy to withdraw from all "external things" into one's "attitude," rich in "external things" but "poor" in one's attitude. It is so terribly easy to say that a robust faith understands the gospel in this way, as though it only appears to deal with externals, though it really does not, but concerns only one's inner attitude, one's "heart." But please, where does the story about poor Lazarus say anything about his "heart"? Who tells us that he was a person who had adopted the right internal attitude toward his poverty? On the contrary, he may have been one of those pushy poor people, since he placed himself at the door of the rich man and would not go away. And who tells us anything about the psyche of the rich man? The really frightening thing about the story is precisely the fact that it is not moralized but simply tells about the poor and the rich, the promise to one and the threat to the other. The objective realities of the story are not dismissed as "externals" but are taken with extreme seriousness. Why did Jesus heal the sick and suffering at all if he was not concerned with "externals"? Why is the kingdom of God spoken of as "the deaf hear and the blind see" (Luke 7:22)? And where do we get the insane arrogance to spiritualize these acts Christ performed with such a straightforward concern for the realities of everyday life?

We simply must stop this shameless, hypocritical spiritualizing of the gospel. Take it as it is or hate it honestly.

Such hatred has not failed to appear precisely when the gospel has been taken at face value. It comes from two different sides.

"Why should we be concerned with a gospel that is for the weak, the low-class, the poor and sick? We are healthy and strong, real men and women who can cope with life. We disdain the mass of Lazaruses. We disdain this 'good news to the poor.' It puts a damper on our pride, our race, our strength. We are rich, and proud of it." This is certainly said honestly. But it is also said far too easily and at the same time is so full of illusions. It is in fact so easy to disdain the mass of Lazaruses. But when you actually encounter a single such person, the jobless Lazarus, the casualty Lazarus, the Lazarus for whose ruin you are guilty, your own begging child as Lazarus, the helpless and despairing mother, the Lazarus who has become a criminal, the godless Lazarus, can you step up to one of these individuals and say, "I despise you, Lazarus. The gospel that brings you joy is a joke to me"? Can you really do that? And if you cannot do it, why then do you only act as though being able to do so is something important?

Or is it not perhaps already a mockery to comfort those who live here in poverty and misery by promising them a better future in another world? Does it not almost seem that we are only trying to distract these unfortunates from rebelling against their fate in this world? As though one pronounces them blessed only to keep them quiet, content with their lot so that they do not bother the others? Is it not simply cynical to speak of heavenly comfort because one is unwilling to give earthly comfort? Is this "good news to the poor" not basically a betrayal of the common people and an attempt to brainwash them? Does it not show that we basically do not take their suffering seriously but cynically hide behind pious rhetoric? Though we would like to deny it, we must sadly acknowledge that it has happened just this way uncountable times, right up to the present moment. But a glance at the Gospels already shows us what is different there. Yes, Jesus pronounces the poor to be blessed (Luke 6:20); but then he heals them too, already in the here and now. Yes, the kingdom of God is present, for the blind see and the lame walk (Luke 7:22). So seriously does he take suffering that he must do something about it in the present. Where Christ is, the power of the demons must be broken. This is why he heals, and this is why he says to his disciples, "the one who believes in me will also do the works that I do and, in fact, will do greater works than these" (John 14:12). The kingdom is not yet here, but it is dawning. Jesus' acts of healing are like lightning that signals the approaching storm, like flashes from the world to come. But now the good news becomes all the more powerful. Blessed are you who weep, for you will laugh, blessed are you who hunger, for you will be filled (Luke 6:21). No cynical putting off with false hopes, but the one grand hope: the new world, the good news, the merciful God, Lazarus in Abraham's bosom, the poor and outcast at home with God—this may indeed sound terribly naïve, plain and simple. But what if it might be true? What if it *is* true? Is it then still naïve? Is it then also against our intellectual and spiritual sophistication? Must we not then open our ears and hear and hear again of the unheard that happens, that Lazarus—yesterday and today—is carried by the angels to be with Abraham? And that the full and satisfied, those who live happily in the grand style, the rich, must endure eternal thirst?

So far we have talked about these two as though they had nothing to do with each other. Obviously, this is not the case. Lazarus lies at the door of the rich man, and it is the poverty of Lazarus that makes the rich man rich, as it is the riches of the rich man that makes poor Lazarus poor. Nothing is said about what the rich man or the poor man have done or what they should have done; the only experience they share in common—and it concerns them both equally—is that they die. This is the odd perspective in which both men come before us: they must both die, and another life awaits them both. And this fact binds them more closely to each other than any moral law that the rich should help the poor. The two are basically already bound together by the common fate that stands before them both. In death, the rich man is no longer rich and the poor man no longer poor. There they are one and the same. And after death something new appears, something about which all the powers of death no longer have any control. This is obviously what the rich man has not seen, that his whole world is a world of death, a world that moves toward death and must do so, a world that finally is in the hands of God. He has not seen that Lazarus is of concern to him because they both must die and live in another world, because, in death and the judgment that follows, they are brothers. This is what he has not seen—that behind him and behind Lazarus stand eternal realities, the world of everlasting reality, the world that is presently silent, invisible, hidden under the veil of purple and the naked body of Lazarus. But they are there, they wait, they will become real. And regarding the seriousness of what is here meant by "eternity," the exchange between the thirsty rich man and Abraham leaves no doubt.

But even though the rich man in torment prays that this eternal reality might already become visible in this world, this does not happen in any other way than through Moses and the prophets or, as we would say today, in the preaching of the church. In their world condemned to death, they have Moses and the prophets; let them hear them. The words of God's incessant command (Matthew 5:17–19), the word of humanity's weakness and misery, condemned to die (Psalm 39:5), the word of God's grace pronounced over the humble, and God's word of judgment pronounced against the mighty, the word of the cross of Christ for the salvation of the poor and lost, the word of curse against those who are full and righteous. Let them hear these words, and let them remember that they all live together with Lazarus in this same world of death, and if they do not hear these words, then they will not hear if one is raised from the dead. They will not be shocked by this most visible of all incursions into their world of death, and they will not perceive. They will resist it and continue business as usual. They will not recognize that the Lazarus before their door is the eternal Lazarus, and they will not notice that in Lazarus they encounter eternity.

And now finally: Who is Lazarus? Who is the rich man, and what, after all, is the rich man supposed to do?

Who is Lazarus? You yourself know: Lazarus is your poor brother or sister, the one who has trouble coping with life, whether the problems are external or internal, the brother or sister who is often foolish, impudent, pushy, godless but still infinitely in need and—whether he or she knows it or not—suffering and longing for the crumbs that may fall from your table. You perhaps have a little self-pity and think you are Lazarus yourself. God alone knows whether you are or not. But you might better always ask whether you might be the rich man. Who is Lazarus? Always the Other, the one who meets you in a thousand despised figures is the crucified Christ himself. Yes, he himself is the eternal Lazarus.

And now we must ask once again, Who is Lazarus? And here at the very end we must with all hesitation consider the final possibility, at the edge of all human and divine possibilities: before God, we are all Lazaruses. Even the rich man is Lazarus. Before God, he too is the poor leper. And it is only when we realize that we are all Lazaruses, because we all live by the grace of God, that we recognize Lazarus in our brother or sister.

Who is the rich man? Our story does not answer this question. Certainly we are not rich. We are not full and satisfied. We do not live happily in the grand style. Really? Are you serious? Not even when you meet Lazarus? Or does Lazarus not appear in your world? Are we really not the rich man? Another story gives us the answer. The story of the rich young man, who was very pious and proper but who still went away sadly when he learned he must turn loose of his riches (Matthew 19:16–22). That is the rich man. And what about us?

And now: what should the rich man do? The answer to this question is found in the story of the Good Samaritan (Luke 10:25–37). In our story only one thing is found: the rich man should see that behind him and Lazarus stands death and that behind Lazarus stand God, Christ, and the everlasting gospel. We are supposed to see this, see poor Lazarus in his off-putting wretchedness and behind him the Christ who has invited him to his supper and pronounces him blessed. Let yourself be seen, poor Lazarus, let yourself be seen, Christ in poor Lazarus. O, that we would want to see.

Once again, I am going through weeks in which I read little in the Bible. I never really know what I should make of this. I don't feel guilty, or that I'm somehow getting behind, and I also know that after a while I will have a craving to plunge back into it. Can one think of this as an entirely "natural" spiritual process? I'm almost inclined to think so.

Dietrich Bonhoeffer to Eberhard Bethge,
Tegel prison, March 19, 1944

Good and Evil

The Bible never wants to make us anxious. God does not want people to be afraid. Not even in view of the Last Judgment. But God has given human beings a revelation so that they might know what their life is and what it means. God lets us know this already in the present so that we may live our lives in sincerity and in the light of the Last Judgment. God lets us know this—only in order that we human beings might find our way to Jesus Christ, that we turn from our own evil way and seek to encounter him, Jesus Christ. God does not want to make us afraid; he sends us the message of judgment only so that we will reach all the more passionately and hungrily for the promise of God's grace, so that we will recognize that we cannot stand before God in our own strength, that when God appears, we would have to disappear, but that in spite of everything God does not want our death but our life.

Christ *judges*. This is an absolutely serious matter. But *Christ* judges, which also must mean, after all, that the Merciful One judges, the one who has lived among publicans and sinners, the one who was tempted just as we are, the one who in his own body has suffered our pain, our anxiety, our desires, the one who knows us and calls us by our name. Christ judges; this means grace is the judge, and forgiveness and love—those who bind themselves to these things are already acquitted. Those who appeal to their own works Christ will judge and condemn according to these works. But we are to rejoice about that day; we are not to worry and tremble but joyfully place ourselves in his hands. "Loving the Last Judgment"—Luther spoke about that.

After all, what is the "good or evil" (2 Corinthian 5:10) about which Christ asks? The "good" is nothing other than seeking God's grace and grasping it; the "evil" is nothing other than the anxiety of wanting to stand before God on our own merits, the will to be righteous in and of ourselves. "Repent"—that refers to nothing else than this turning, this complete reorientation away from our own works and to God's mercy and taking our stand there. "Repent, repent"—these joyful words ring out to us throughout the Bible. "Turn back"—to what? To the eternal grace of God, to the One who does not abandon us, to the One whose heart is broken about us, because this God loves us, his creatures, in a way that can never be measured.

The Word of God Needs No Decoration

We want to speak of how our God can be praised and worshipped through song and music. The God of Jesus Christ and his worship in the music of his church—that is what we wish to talk about.

Those among us who can remember the first time they were in church will certainly recall that what impressed them more than anything else was the thunderous, unforgettable strains of the organ. Part anxiety, part awe, part terror, part inner attraction—this is the way it must be in heaven, this is the way the angels and departed saints above must sing before God's throne—something like this must be the way to describe the turmoil of our souls in their first encounter with the music of the church. What soul does not still resonate with its echoes?

But perhaps there are also several among our number who from their childhood belonged to that Reformed Church in which no organ or other musical instrument was permitted because it did not want to minimize the glory of the proclaimed word of God and the Holy Scripture or cover it over by any human addition. And such a person may then have perceived the sound of the organ as one of those forbidden human attempts to proclaim God's glory in some other way than through God's word. Such a person might still feel a deep, quiet shudder at the music of the church.

The story is told that the great Italian Renaissance poet Petrarch once looked out over the flourishing countryside from a peak in the mountains of northern Italy and was overcome with the feeling: God, how beautiful, how beautiful is this world. But in the very next moment he crossed himself, opened his breviary, and began to pray. This is the person who backs away in dread from the beauty of this world and flees in anxiety from its splendor. He does not want to love the beauty of this world more than the One who created it. How terribly dangerous it is for anyone who has stood in St. Peter's in Rome to hear and love the heavenly voices of the Sistine Choir—and not to love the very voice of God as it sounds forth from the language of the Bible. How close to blasphemy to use such rich, splendid accomplishments of human art to celebrate the memory of the man who wore carpenter's clothes and spoke the clear and simple language of everyday life; this might obscure the poverty and lowliness of Jesus Christ.

That we love the creation more than God, this is the deep danger and temptation of all those who want to love music for God's sake. Of course, we do not want to look disdainfully on those others who want to avoid such dangers by having only the word of God read in church. There is great seriousness in this approach, much knowledge of the uniqueness and exclusiveness, the austerity of the divine revelation, for which there can be no replacement. The word of God needs no decoration.

We want to keep this firmly in mind: the word of God, as found in the Bible and as it sounds forth to us in the proclamation of the gospel, needs no decoration. It is its own decoration, its own glory, its own beauty. This is certainly true. But as is especially true of human beauty, the word of God cannot withdraw itself from the decoration of those who love it. As is true of decorating that which is truly beautiful, the decoration of the word of God can only consist of making its own inner beauty shine forth all the more gloriously—nothing alien to it, nothing false, nothing artificial, no kitschy trinkets and no cosmetics, nothing that covers up its own beauty but only what reveals and brings it to light.

And those who love this word of God that has sounded forth for two thousand years have not let themselves be talked out of contributing the most beautiful thing they could as its decoration. And their most beautiful work could be nothing else than something invisible, namely, an obedient heart, but from this obedient heart there springs forth the visible work, the audible song in praise of God and Jesus Christ.

Incidentally, I'm now reading the Bible through, starting at the beginning and now up to the book of Job, which I especially love. For years I've read the Psalter daily; there is no other book I know and love so well as this one. I can no longer read Psalms 3, 47, 70, and others without hearing them in the music of Heinrich Schütz. Knowing them in this way belongs to the greatest enrichments of my life.

Dietrich Bonhoeffer to his parents,
Tegel prison, May 15, 1943

Praying the Psalms

From ancient times the church has attributed special significance to unison congregational prayer in the words of the Psalter. To the present moment, many churches begin every worship service in this way. Among us the practice has fallen into widespread disuse, and we must first find our way back to an appreciation of psalmic prayer. The Psalter holds a unique place within the whole of Holy Scripture. It is God's word, and at the same time it is, with few exceptions, the prayers of human beings. How is this to be understood? How can God's word be at the same time prayer to God?

All those who begin to pray the psalms not only are aware of this question but also make a personal discovery. At first they attempt to repeat them as their own individual prayer. But soon they come to passages that they do not believe they can pray as their personal prayer. We think, for example, of the psalms protesting our own innocence, of the imprecatory psalms, and of some of the psalms of the sufferers. All the same, these prayers are words of Holy Scripture that cannot be easily dismissed as outdated, as obsolete, or as "preliminary stages of religion." They do not want their own views to dominate Scripture, and yet recognize that they cannot pray in these words. They can read them as prayers of someone else, listen to them, be surprised by or take offense at them, but can neither pray them nor eliminate them from Holy Scripture. Of course, in almost every instance one could say that we should stick to the psalms that we can understand and pray and that reading the other psalms might teach us just to leave the difficult and incomprehensible parts of the Bible alone and stay with the clear texts we can understand. The fact is, however, the problem we have pointed to may provide us the standpoint from which we may have our first glance into the real mystery of the Psalter. Praying the psalms that are difficult to let pass over our lips, those that bring us up short and even horrify us, gives us a premonition that here someone else is praying, someone different from ourselves, that the one who here protests his innocence, who calls for God's judgment, the one who has come into such deep suffering, is none other than—Jesus Christ himself. He is the one who prays not only in these difficult psalms but in the Psalter as a whole. From the very beginning, the New Testament and the church have recognized and testified to this. The human being Jesus Christ, who was spared no distress, no sickness, no suffering, and who was the altogether innocent and righteous one, it is he who prays in the Psalter through the mouth of his church. The Psalter is the Prayer Book of Jesus Christ in the most real sense. He prayed the Psalter; now it has become his prayer for all time. Can we now understand how it could be that the Psalter is at one and the same time prayer to God and still God's own word precisely because it is the praying Christ who here encounters us? Jesus Christ prays the Psalter in his church. To be sure, his church prays too, individual worshippers pray, but they truly pray to the extent that Jesus Christ prays within them; they pray not in their own name but in the name of Jesus Christ. They do not pray from the natural longing of their own hearts but pray from within the humanity of Jesus Christ they have assumed; they pray on the basis of the prayer of the human being Jesus Christ. On this basis alone they can pray with the promise they will be heard. Christ has become our intercessor.

The Psalter is the prayer of Christ for his church, in which he stands in for us and prays in our behalf. Now, since Christ is with the Father, it is the new humanity of Christ that prays, the body of Christ on earth that continues his prayer to the end of time. It is not the individual Christian to whom the prayer belongs—no, it belongs to the whole body of Christ. Everything expressed in the Psalter lives in the body of Christ as a whole; no individual can completely grasp all this and name it as belonging to him or her personally. This is why praying the Psalms belongs in a special way to the community. If a particular verse or psalm is not my own prayer, it is still the prayer of someone else in the Christian fellowship, just as it is surely the prayer of the truly human being Jesus Christ and his body on earth.

In the Psalter we learn to pray on the basis of Christ's own prayer. The Psalter as such is the great school of prayer. In the *first* place, we learn here what it means to pray: to pray on the basis of the word of God, to pray on the basis of promises. Christian prayer stands on the firm ground of the revealed word and has nothing to do with vague, selfish desires. We pray on the basis of the prayer of the true man Jesus Christ. This is what the Scripture means when it says that the Holy Spirit prays within us and for us, that Christ prays for us, that now we can approach God directly in prayer in the name of Jesus Christ.

In the *second* place, we learn, by praying the Psalter, what we should pray for. Just as surely as the range of the prayers of the Psalter goes far beyond the experience of any individual, we still pray the whole prayer of Christ in faith, the prayer of the one who was the truly human being and who alone has taken into his life the full range of the experiences of this prayer. May we then pray even the imprecatory psalms? We may not do this as sinners who associate evil desires with these prayers for revenge; but as those in whom Christ dwells—the one who has taken all God's judgment upon himself, the one who thus, as the one who is himself struck by the judgment of God, could forgive his enemies, the one who himself suffered the divine vengeance that his enemies might go free—as members of the body of this Jesus Christ, we too may pray even these psalms, through Jesus Christ and out of the heart of Jesus Christ.

May we identify ourselves with the psalmist and thus call ourselves innocent, pious, and righteous? We may not do this as those who claim these qualities for ourselves, we cannot do it as the prayer of our own perverse hearts, but we may and should do it from the sinless and pure heart of Jesus Christ and from the innocence of Jesus Christ, in which he lets us participate by faith; we may and should pray the psalms of innocence as Christ's prayer for us and his gift to us. These psalms too belong to us through him.

And how can we pray those prayers of inexpressible suffering and misery, we who have hardly begun to grasp, even from a distance, what is meant here? Not in order to identify ourselves sympathetically with something that we have not experienced in our own hearts, not in order to lament something about ourselves, but because all this suffering became true and real in Jesus Christ, because the human being Jesus Christ suffered sickness, pain, shame, and death, and because in his suffering and death all humanity has suffered and died. This is why we can and should pray these psalms.

In the *third* place, praying the psalms teaches us to pray as a community. The body of Christ prays, and as an individual I recognize that my own prayer is only a tiny fragment of the whole prayer of the community. I learn to pray the prayer of the body of Christ as my own prayer, to pray along with the church as a whole. This lifts me beyond my own personal concerns and lets me pray unselfishly. Many psalms were in all probability prayed responsively. The formal parallelism of many psalms, that is, that striking repetition of the same substance in other words in the second half of the verse, not only is a literary form but has a churchly-theological meaning. It would be worthwhile to study this subject very thoroughly. Psalm 5 can be read as a very clear example of this. There are always two voices that alternate in bringing one and the same concern before God in prayer. Should this not be an indication that the one who prays never prays alone but that there is always a second person, an other, a fellow Christian, a member of the body of Christ—yes, Jesus Christ himself must be praying alongside the one who prays, so that the prayer of the individual may truly be a prayer? Should we not also learn something from the repetition of the same substance, which finally in Psalm 119 intensifies in an almost unapproachable, unexplainable simplicity that would like to go on forever? Is not this a signal that each and every prayer verse wants to impress itself into the depths of our hearts in a way that can be achieved only by unceasing repetition—and finally not even that!? Does this not teach us that prayer is not a matter of the incidental pouring out of the needs and joys of the individual human heart but the constant, steady process of learning, allowing oneself to appropriate and have impressed in one's memory the will of God as revealed in Jesus Christ? The deeper we penetrate into the Psalms and the more often we ourselves have prayed them, the simpler and richer our own prayer will become.

Faith does not depend on dead letters but on the living Lord, who places himself before us as one whose commanding word transcends all doubts about the Bible and its stories.

An outline for a catechism by Dietrich Bonhoeffer and Franz Hildebrandt, 1932

I Will Not Forget Thy Words—Psalm 119

With my whole heart I seek you;
do not let me stray from
your commandments.
(v. 10)

Those who have accepted God's word must begin to seek God; they can do no other. The more clearly and deeply God's word reveals itself to us, the more lively becomes the longing for the complete clarity and unfathomable depths of God himself. By the gift of his word, God drives us to seek knowledge that is ever richer, a gift that is ever more glorious. God wants no false modesty. The more we receive, the more we must seek God, and the more we seek, the more we will receive from God. "To those who have, more will be given" (Matthew 13:12). God wants to glorify himself completely in us, to be revealed in all the richness of divine glory. Of course, we can seek God nowhere else but in his word; but this word is living and inexhaustible—for the living God is himself present in it. When we have been struck by God's word, we can say, "I seek you with my whole heart." With half our heart we might seek an idol but never the one true God. God needs the whole heart. God wants nothing (no thing) from us but wants us, ourselves, our whole self. God's word has said this to us. This is why we seek him with our whole heart. We still have only one thing to be concerned about—that we might stray from the way we have begun, from the commandments we have learned. The psalmist, praying, speaks of "straying." He no longer thinks of willful, intentional violation of known divine commands. But how easily we go astray; when evil clouds our view, we wander off on bypaths, no longer know which way to turn, cannot find our own way back to God's commandments. We must pray every day for God to preserve us from the sin of straying, from unintended sin (Numbers 15:22ff.), for once we have wandered off unawares into the paths of evil, we begin rather quickly to enjoy these paths, and what began as unintended straying turns into an evil will. But those who seek God with their whole hearts will not go astray.

I treasure your word in my heart,
so that I may not sin against you.
(v. 11)

When God's word comes to us, it wants to find fertile soil in which to grow. It does not want to be left on the hard path. It is a great miracle that the eternal word of the almighty God seeks in me a place to dwell, wants to be received by me, like seed in soil. God's word is sown not in my intellect but in my heart. Not as something to be analyzed to death but as something kept alive in our hearts like the word of a beloved friend or member of the family that rests gently in our heart even when we are not consciously aware of it—this is the goal of the word that comes to us from the mouth of God. If I only keep God's word in my intellect, then my thoughts will often be occupied with other matters, and what God has to say to me will miss its target. So we are never finished with God's word when we have merely read the Bible; it must penetrate deep within us, dwell in us, like the Most Holy Place within the sanctuary, so that we do not go astray in our thoughts, words, and deeds. It is often better to read only a little in Scripture and wait until it has penetrated deep within us than to know a lot about God's word but not "treasure it in our hearts."

I will meditate on your precepts
and fix my eyes on your ways.
(v. 15)

There is no standing still. Every gift, every increment of knowledge and insight I receive only drives me deeper into the word of God. For God's word I need time. To rightly understand the commands of God, I must often ponder their meaning for a long time. Nothing could be more wrong than the kind of intense activity or emotional high that denies the value of hard thinking and reflection. Such engagement with the Bible is also not just the business of those who are especially called to this vocation but the business of anyone who wants to walk in God's ways.

Admittedly, it is often the case that God calls us to act quickly with no delay; but God also calls us to quietness and meditation. So I am often both permitted and required to halt for hours or days over one and the same word until I am enlightened with the right insight. No one is so advanced that he or she no longer needs to do this. No one may believe that he or she has been excused from this because of too many other active responsibilities. God's word claims my time. God himself has entered into time and now wills that I give him my time. To be Christian is not something that can be handled in a moment, but demands time. God has given us the Scripture, from which we are to discern God's will. The Scripture wants to be read and thought about, every day afresh. God's word is not the sum of a few general statements that I can call to memory anytime I want but is the word of God directed to me, new every day, in the inexhaustibly rich process of interpretation. Meditation, that is, prayerful reflection on the Scripture and its interpretation, is indispensable to the one who honestly seeks God's commands and not merely his or her own ideas. Theologians who do not practice both prayerful reflection and practical interpretation deny their office. But to all Christians the time needed for this is given if they really seek it. Meditation means to take God's word for me prayerfully to heart; interpretation means to recognize and understand God's word in the Scripture as God's word. We cannot have one without the other. Rather, both are included in the kind of thinking that must be practiced daily.

I will delight in your statutes;
I will not forget your word.
(v. 16)

Why is it that my thoughts so quickly wander away from God's word and that the word I need is often not there when I need it? Do I ever forget to eat or drink or sleep? Why then do I forget God's word? Because I am not yet able to say with the psalmist, "I will delight in your statutes." I do not forget that in which I delight. Whether or not I forget something is (not) a matter (of my intellect but) of the whole person, a matter of the heart. That on which I depend, body and soul, is something I cannot forget. The more I begin to love God's statutes written in creation and Scripture, the more they will be present to me in every moment. Only love keeps one from forgetting.

Because God has spoken to us in history, and that means in the past, it is necessary to remember; a necessary daily exercise is to repeat what has been learned. Every day we must go back afresh to the saving acts of God in order to be able to go forward. This is why the Scripture warns us constantly and urgently not to forget. "Do not forget all his benefits" (Psalm 103:2). "Take care that you do not forget the Lord, who brought you out of the land of Egypt, out of the house of bondage" (Deuteronomy 6:12; read the whole chapter!). "Remember Jesus Christ" (2 Timothy 2:8). It is by memory and repetition that faith and obedience live. Memory becomes the power of the present because it is the living God who once acted for me and who today reassures me of his saving act. The past in and of itself is of no concern. But because something happened "for me" in the past, that makes all the difference today, the past act becomes present for the one who grasps this "for me" by faith, "for that phrase 'for you' calls for truly believing hearts" (Luther).

Because my salvation does not lie in me, in my own self, but is something that happened in the world outside my psyche, because my righteousness is the righteousness of Jesus Christ alone, because this can only be proclaimed to me in the word—this is why memory and recalling into the present are necessary for the sake of the blessing; this is why forgetting means the same as falling away from the faith.

In the daily remembering of Jesus Christ, however, it is pledged to me that God has loved me from all eternity and has not forgotten me (Isaiah 49:14–16). But if I know that God does not forget me because of his love for me, then I rejoice and am filled with new love for God's faithfulness in his word, and I learn to say, "I will not forget your word."

Deal bountifully with your servant,
so that I may live and observe your word.
(v. 17)

I too ask for life, as the slave asks his master. Life is the good gift of God. Life is not a means to some other good but is itself fulfillment. God created us that we might live, he reconciled and redeemed us that we might live. God is not interested in the triumph of ideas on a battlefield of corpses. Ideas are there for the sake of life, not life for the sake of ideas. Where life itself is made into an idea, there the real created and redeemed life is more utterly destroyed than through any other idea. God's goal with us is life. If life becomes the means to an end, then a contradiction steps into life that lets it become misery. Then the goal, the good, is sought beyond life itself, a transaction that can only be paid for by denying the goodness of life itself. That is the situation in which we find ourselves before we accept life in God; we have been taught to call this situation good. We become haters and disdainers of life, and lovers and worshippers of ideas.

I ask God for the good gift of life. Only the life that God gives is blessing. All other life is misery. Only life lived from God is itself goal and fulfillment, only there is the contradiction overcome between life as it is and life as it should be.

Life is the time of grace; death is judgment. This is why life is the divine gift, because time is given me for the grace of God. Such time is present so long as the word of God is present with me. To hold fast to this word is to say yes to living out one's life as from God. God's word is not beyond life, it does not demote life from end to means, but protects life from deteriorating in the face of contradictions, from the tyranny of ideas. God's word is the fulfillment of life itself, beyond which there is no further goal. This is why I ask God for the gift of life, the life that has been wasted away before him, like the life of a slave to his master, and that is fulfilled by keeping the word of God.

Open my eyes, so that I may behold wondrous things out of your law.
(v. 18)

The one whose eyes have been opened by God looks into a world of wonders. That which previously looked dead to me is full of life, that which was filled with contradictions is resolved in a higher unity, the severe demand becomes a gracious commandment. In the midst of human words I hear God's eternal word, in past history I recognize God who is present and his saving work in me. The tender words of encouragement become a new claim of God upon my life, the unbearable burden becomes the easy yoke (Matthew 11:30). *The* great miracle in the law of God is the revelation of the Lord Jesus Christ. Through him the word comes to life, the contradictions are resolved, the obvious receives an unfathomable depth. O Lord, open my eyes.

I am a guest on the earth;
do not hide your commandments from me.
(v. 19)

For the one who has become a foreigner on this earth according to the will and call of God, there is truly only one thought that can fill him or her with deepest anxiety. This thought is that the time may come when one no longer recognizes God's will, no longer knows what God requires from him or her. Of course, in our personal life's choices or in God's actions in history, God is often hidden; it is not this that fills us with anxiety. But that the obvious command of God may veil itself from us so that we no longer recognize from the word of God what we should do—this is a severe ordeal. In the midst of the joyful confidence of God's command, this fear falls upon us: what if one day God decides to hide his command from me? I would have to plunge headlong into the abyss of nothingness, I would stumble at my first step, I would have to come to ruin and grief in a foreign land, a long, long way from home. Or—I might as well go ahead and ask myself now—am I perhaps already living so much within the framework of my own principles that I might not even notice if one day God should withdraw his living word from me? Perhaps I would just continue living by my own rules, but God's command would no longer be with me. God's command is God's personal word to me for this day for my life here and now; it is, to be sure, not today one thing and something else tomorrow that God wants of me. In itself, God's command is one. But the decisive difference is whether I obey God or live by my own principles. If I am satisfied to live by my own principles, then I cannot understand the psalmist's prayer. But if I allow God himself to direct my way, then I am totally dependent on the grace that reveals itself to me or withholds itself from me, then I tremble at every word I receive from the mouth of God, tremble at the prospect of the next word and whether I will be maintained in grace. Then I am bound by grace in all my ways and decisions, and no false certainty can lead me astray from this living communion with God.

The cry that God may not hide his command from me can only come from the heart of the one who knows God's commands. There is no doubt: God has given us his commands so that we might know them, and we have no excuse, as though we did not know what God requires of us. God does not let us live in insoluble conflicts, does not make our lives into ethical tragedies, but lets us know his will, demands that it be fulfilled, and punishes the disobedient. Things here are much simpler than we like to believe. It's not that we do not know God's commands but that we do not do them—and then, of course, as a result of such disobedience, gradually lose the capacity to recognize God's command for what it is. The text here does not say that God hides his commands from us; instead God is implored not to hide his commands. In God's freedom and wisdom the possibility is always there that God could withdraw the grace of his command, but this means for us not resignation but rather the urgent and persistent prayer "Do not hide your commands from me."

Language

In the Protestant church, the church where the word of God is proclaimed, language is no formality, no matter of externals. I understand very well your continual irritation at the way we so casually and as a matter of course speak about things that a human being ought barely to be able to utter at all. You are also quite right when you say that words such as "sin," "grace," and "forgiveness" receive an entirely different tone, an entirely different weight, when they are spoken by someone who otherwise never says them. The word that ventures into the light from a long period of silence weighs more than the same word in the mouth of a chatterbox. I will also grant you that certain words have been worn out and should never be used at all. In any case, it has often been (rightly) said that there should be less preaching so that the word might actually make a deeper impression.

But that too is, after all, certainly "tendentious," naïve, and artificial. Time and again in the exercise of pastoral care, we pastors experience the reality that a word from the mouth of someone who is sick, impoverished, or lonely is something entirely different from quoting it ourselves. Often enough, we are hesitant to cite biblical texts ourselves, so as not to seem to be there only in our official, routinized capacity. But we also know that we are under a mandate to speak, and often dare not keep silent even when we would prefer to do so. Just once place yourself in our shoes, we who from dawn to dusk are supposed to deal with the greatest words in the world "because it's our job," reading, studying, praying, teaching, baptizing, consoling, burying, preaching. We cannot then be grateful enough when someone points out to us where we are doing it wrong, perhaps even with all our subjective involvement still just lapsing into the recitation of empty words. But above all, we would like to know how we can do it better. It would not help to resolve on some sort of drastic surgery, striking from our vocabulary, for instance, all such words as "cross," "sin," or "grace." To begin with, "cross" could not be replaced by "guillotine," since in fact it was on a cross that Jesus died. And using a word such as "feeding trough" instead of "manger" might seem to help for a moment, but by the third or fourth time one has heard it, it too has been used up. Of course, there are words, especially our favorite expressions we have sought out or even invented, that one can and should eliminate, but if we speak at all, we must use some form of words. Whether the "everyday language of the average person" is the right approach or not I do not claim to know. Luther's own language was certainly not this. I doubt that one should consciously try to develop some particular style of speech. It is not helpful that Christianity is two thousand years old and has developed its own language. In my opinion, we should stay with the plain language of the Bible in order to enter into conversation with what it has to say (just as one wants "water and not juice" for ordinary daily use). But it depends on the depth from which these words come and the context in which they stand.

Incidentally, I need to say the following personal word to you: the heavy air raids, especially the last one, in which the aerial explosions in the district blew out the windows and knocked the bottles and medicine out of the cabinets and shelves, have made me think. I lay in the darkness on the floor and did not have much hope to come through it, and was brought back to the basics of prayer and Bible.

Dietrich Bonhoeffer to Eberhard Bethge,
Tegel prison, November 26, 1943

Word and Deed

In a world in which deeds speak their own language in such an overwhelming way, what is the word of the church supposed to be? Has it not become superfluous? Should we not ourselves simply fall in line with these deeds and, in place of so many words, just contribute our own deeds? Deeds are credible. Should we complain about how deeds come about in this world? That deeds take matters into their own hands? That here the applicable watchword is simply that God helps those who help themselves? It is precisely as we stand in the midst of deeds that we ask for a clarifying word—otherwise we cannot carry on.

Deeds make their own point. They roll wordlessly over everything weaker than they are. They knock it down and trample on it. Petty critiques are crushed by the force of the deed itself. This is the inherent law of the deed. Only one is greater than the deed: the one who grants it. Every deed knows this, that it is not its own master but is permitted and given. It should render praise to the one who grants it. Whether it does that or not is decided by its stance toward the word of God. The word of God is there, and is the only thing over which the deed has no power.

Human capacities for the word of God may be small and weak, so that they are broken and wiped out along with all else that is purely human. The word alone endures forever. It challenges every deed without fear, for it is eternal, invulnerable, almighty. Its advocates may not be worthy of it; then they must disappear. The word, however, forces its own path wherever it pleases, and chooses its own hearers as it pleases, for it is God's own word. The poverty of the word. The same God, who allows and grants great deeds, who visibly and yet incomprehensibly gives and takes away, wants to rescue humanity and grant it eternal salvation. In the deeds themselves God remains silent, but he reveals himself to those he wishes to save, the ones who are to find him. This revelation happens in the poverty of the word, for God wants to be *believed* and *trusted.* God does not want to compel belief by a miracle but wants to speak to the heart by the word and lead it to a freely chosen faith.

When we ask ourselves in troubled times what, after all, is still there after all the excitement, all our thoughts going this way and that, all our worries and fears, all the wishes and hopes we make for ourselves—if we are willing to let the Bible give us its answer, this is what is said to us: Out of all this there finally remains only one thing, namely, the love we have in our thoughts, worries, wishes, and hopes. Everything else comes to an end, passes away, everything we have thought about and longed for out of love. All ideas, knowledge, all speaking without love come to an end—only love never comes to an end.

Dietrich Bonhoeffer in a sermon
on 1 Corinthians 13:8–12,
October 28, 1934

Word of God and the Creeds

The *church* is gathered around word and sacrament: a fellowship of faith, of worship, of life. It is built alone on the word of God.

Theology is the inflection of the church's faith under the comprehensive and ordered knowledge of the word of God in its contextual and concrete form, as guided by the creedal statements of the church. Theology serves the authentic proclamation of the word in the church and the building up of the community in conformity with the word of God.

The essence of the church is not to practice theology but to *believe* and *obey* the word of God. But because it has pleased God to make himself known in the *spoken human word* and because this word is subject to distortion and dilution by human ideas and opinions, the community needs clarity about what constitutes true and false preaching—it needs theology not as an end in itself but as a means to help keep its proclamation authentic and combat false preaching. In times of testing and temptation the church is called in a special way to such maturity. The *word of God* is the only norm and rule of all true Christian knowledge. The *creedal confession* is the exposition and inflection of the word of God for a particular time and danger and is itself subject to the word of God. *Theology* is the exposition of the church's confession from particular points of view and with a constant testing of the confession by Scripture. *Faith* comes only by the preaching of the word of God (Romans 10:17); it does not need theology, but authentic preaching needs both the creeds and theology. Faith, called into being by Christian preaching, turns to the Scripture and the creeds for its confirmation and thus engages in theology.

What importance do the *theological disciplines* have for the church? Is it not enough just to know the Bible? What need is there for dogmatics? For church history? For practical theology? What is the connection between congregational life and theology? One cannot understand the Bible apart from the basic teachings of the church, that is, dogmatics. One cannot engage in dogmatics without study of the Bible. One cannot overlook the reality that between us and the Bible there stands a *church* that has a history. Practical theology means to act *today*, but to do so under the word of Scripture, the creeds, history, and theology.

My activities in recent times have been located mainly in the secular sector; they have repeatedly made me think. I am surprised that I go for days without reading the Bible and that I can in fact live this way. If I were to force myself to read the Bible anyway, I would perceive it not as obedience but as autosuggestion. I understand that such autosuggestion could be and is a real help, but I am afraid this path leads to the perversion of an authentic experience and so ultimately does not help. When I do come back to the Bible again, it is fresh and exhilarating as never before, and I want to go out and preach. I know that I need only look into the books I've written myself to find what can be said against all this. Nor am I trying simply to justify myself but to recognize that "spiritually" I have had far richer times. But I feel growing within myself a resistance to everything "religious"—often to the point of an instinctive disgust, which certainly cannot be good. By nature, I'm not a "religious person." But I must continually think about God, about Christ, and my thoughts are often concerned with authenticity, life, freedom, compassion. Do you understand? None of these are new thoughts or insights, but since I believe that here I'm about to break through the knots, I'm letting things take their course and not defending myself. So this is the way I understand even my present activity in the secular sector.

Dietrich Bonhoeffer to Eberhard Bethge
during the time of the conspiracy,
in the train to Munich, June 25, 1942

Old Testament and New Testament

I am noticing more and more how much I think and feel in terms of the Old Testament; in the past few months I have read more Old Testament than New Testament. Only when one knows the inexpressibleness of the name of God can one then venture to speak the name of Jesus Christ. Only when one so loves this life and this earth that everything appears to end and be lost with it is one permitted to believe in the resurrection of the dead and the new world. Only when one accepts the validity of God's law for oneself is one permitted to speak of grace. And only when the wrath and vengeance of God on his enemies is real can our hearts be moved by forgiveness and love of enemies. Whoever wants to live and feel too quickly and too directly in terms of the New Testament is, in my opinion, not truly Christian. One cannot speak the ultimate word before the penultimate. We live in the penultimate and believe in the ultimate. Such ideas would give goose pimples to Lutherans (so-called) and Pietists, but this is nonetheless the right way to see the matter. In *The Cost of Discipleship* I only hinted at these ideas (in the first chapter) and did not later pursue them [see DBW 4]. The consequences are very far-reaching—for the Catholic problem, for the concept of church office, for the use of the Bible, to mention only a few—but especially for ethics. Why is it that in the Old Testament lies are told vigorously and often for the honor of God (I have collected a list of passages), people are killed, betrayed, and robbed, marriages are broken up, and even prostitution, doubt, blasphemy, and cursing are practiced while none of this is found in the New Testament? An "elementary stage of religion"? That is a very naïve statement—after all, it is one and the same God.

In distinction from other oriental religions, the Old Testament faith is no religion of redemption. Christianity, on the other hand, is always described as a religion of redemption. Do we not find here a cardinal error by which Christ is separated from the Old Testament and interpreted in terms of the myth of redemption? To the objection that, in the Old Testament too, redemption (from Egypt and later from Babylon; cf. Deutero-Isaiah) plays a decisive role, it must be pointed out that here it is a matter of *historical* redemption, that is, *this side* of the boundary of death, whereas everywhere else the goal of the redemption myth is the overcoming of death itself. Israel is redeemed from Egypt so that it can live in this world as the people of God. The redemption myths seek, in a nonhistorical way, an eternal redemption after death. Sheol (the netherworld) and Hades are not, in the Old Testament, metaphysical conceptions but the pictures by means of which what "has been" on earth is portrayed as still existing, certainly, but only as a shadow existence with regard to the present world. Of course it is said that the important thing is that in Christianity the resurrection is proclaimed and that thereby a real religion of redemption came into being. The emphasis is now on the world beyond death. And precisely here is where the mistake and the danger lie. Redemption now means redemption from worries, troubles, anxieties, and longings, from sin and death into a better world beyond this one. But is this really supposed to be the essential thing about the proclamation of Christ in the Gospels and Paul? I dispute this. The Christian hope of the resurrection is distinguished from mythological ideas by the fact that human beings are directed to their authentic life on this earth in an even more pronounced manner than in the Old Testament. Christian believers, in contrast to believers in the redemption myth, have no final flight into eternity from the responsibilities and difficulties of this world but like Christ must savor and fulfill this earthly life completely ("My God, why have you forsaken me?" Mark 15:34). Only by their doing so is the Crucified and Risen One with them; only in this way are they crucified and risen with Christ. This world may not be canceled out too quickly. Old Testament and New Testament are united on this point. Redemption myths originate in the human boundary experiences. But Christ apprehends us in the midst of life, not only at its edges.

The God who is with us is the God who forsakes us (Mark 15:34)! The God who lets us live in the world without making use of the God hypothesis is the God before whom we constantly stand. Before God and with God we live without God. God allows himself to be edged out of the world and onto the cross. God is weak and powerless in the world; precisely in this way and only in this way is God with us and helps us. Matthew 8:17 makes it crystal clear that Christ does not help us because he is the Almighty One but by virtue of his weakness, his sufferings! This is the decisive difference between Christian faith and all religions. It is human religiosity that points us in our distress to the power of God in the world, and God becomes the deus ex machina. The Bible points human beings to the weakness and suffering of God. Only the suffering God can help.

"So, could you not stay awake with me one hour?" asks Jesus in Gethsemane (Matthew 26:40). This is the reversal of everything the religious person expects from God. Human beings are called to suffer with God at the hands of a godless world. They must therefore really live in the godless world and must not try to conceal or explain their own godlessness by some religious covering. They must live in a "worldly" manner and precisely in this way participate in God's own suffering. They are granted permission to live in this "worldly" way, that is, as freed from false religious commitments and constraints. To be Christian does not mean to live in a specified religious way, based on a particular method by which one makes oneself into a particular kind of person (whether sinner, penitent, or saint), but it means to be human, not a particular human type; Christ creates true humanity in us. It is not religious acts that make one Christian but participation in the suffering of Christ in worldly life.

You suppose the Bible does not have much to say about health, strength, happiness, and the like. I have thought this through again very carefully. At least for the Old Testament, this characterization just does not fit. In the Old Testament the theological middle term between God and human happiness, so far as I can tell, is that of blessing. Admittedly, the Old Testament does not have much to say about the happiness of, for example, the patriarchs but speaks of God's blessing, the comprehensive term for all the good things of this earth. This blessing means claiming earthly life for God and includes all God's promises. Thus it would fit the usual spiritualizing interpretation of the New Testament to regard the Old Testament concept of blessing as superseded by the New Testament understanding.

But should we oppose the Old Testament blessing to the cross? This would be to make the cross, or suffering as such, into a general principle. Anyway, in the Old Testament those who are blessed must also suffer much (Abraham, Isaac, Jacob, Joseph), but this never leads to the contrasting of happiness and suffering, blessing and cross, as mutually exclusive alternatives (anymore than this happens in the New Testament). In this regard the difference between Old Testament and New Testament is rather that in the Old Testament blessing includes the cross, in the New Testament the cross includes blessing.

The New Testament is the testimony to the fulfillment of the Old Testament promise in Christ. It is not a book of eternal truths, doctrines, norms, or myths but is a single united witness to the incarnation of God in the man Jesus

Christ. It is as a whole and in all its parts nothing else than this witness to Christ—his life, death, and resurrection. This Christ is witnessed to not as the Eternal in the temporal, as Meaning in the accidental course of things, as the Essence of the transient! Rather, Christ is testified to as the simply unique human being in whom God has become human, the one who died and was raised from the dead, and this unique, once-for-all character of the Christ event in history fills the whole New Testament. Here there is no distinction between *didactic* texts (in the Epistles or in the sayings of Jesus) and the *narrative* texts. Both are in the same way testimony to the unique Christ, so their relationship to each other is not, for example, that the didactic texts express general truths about Christ whereas a miracle story reports an incidental, unique happening—both in the same way testify to the uniqueness of Jesus Christ, who entered fully into history. In the miracle story just as in a parable or a command in the Sermon on the Mount, it is Christ himself who is proclaimed, not this or that truth or doctrine about him or some particular action he performed. The testimony is given to "the Christ, the whole Christ, and nothing but the Christ." Christ is the one who does the miracle, tells the parable, gives the command, and by miracle, parable, command, or teaching he wants one and the same thing—to bind human beings to himself as the unique one manifest in history. This is the common denominator of the New Testament as a whole, this is the one fact to which the whole New Testament bears witness.

In precisely the same way, a Pauline text is not essentially a statement of some theological truth—although it is that too—but is the unique testimony to the unique Christ. One might say that in the Gospels it is the miracle of the incarnation, the manifestation of God in human form, that is more viable whereas in the Epistles emphasis is placed on the miracle of the cross and resurrection, but it is still the case that in the Gospels the whole Christ as the Crucified and Risen One and in the Epistles the whole Christ as the Incarnate One are testified to as the unique act of God.

It could appear that didactic texts can more easily be translated into present meaning than narrative texts about events in history. But here again a false distinction is made, as though the Bible contained some items that are eternal truths that represent teaching valid for all time whereas the narratives of events in history have only a relative, time-conditioned validity. The New Testament, in both its didactive and narrative parts, is testimony; it is not something in and of itself but testifies to something beyond itself. Its value is not what it is in itself but only as witness to Christ. It claims nothing for itself but points beyond itself. Its words and statements are not true, eternal, and valid in themselves but only as they testify to Christ—this means they want to let Christ alone be the truth. The whole New Testament in all its parts wants to be understood as testimony—not as a book of wisdom or doctrines, not as a book of eternal truths, but as a book of unique testimonies to a unique once-for-all fact that has occurred in history. It is the "joyful shout": *This Jesus is the Christ!* "To this man you should point and say, 'Here is God' " (Luther).

The situation as such, that is, the individual moment, is in many ways not any different from being someplace else: I read, reflect, work, write, walk back and forth—and even without rubbing myself raw against the walls like the polar bear. It's just a matter of concentrating on what one still has and can do—and this is still very much—and keeping in check those thoughts about what one does not have and the resentment and anxiety about the whole situation. And what the Bible and Luther mean by the ordeal of temptation and testing [die Anfechtung] has certainly never become so clear to me as here. Quite without any recognizable physical or psychological basis, the peace and composure that have carried one along are suddenly shaken, and the heart becomes, as Jeremiah describes it, the devious and perverse thing that no one can understand (Jeremiah 17:9). One feels it as really breaking in from outside oneself, as evil powers that want to rob one of what is most important. But these experiences too are good and necessary; one learns to understand better one's human existence.

Dietrich Bonhoeffer to his parents,
Tegel prison, May 15, 1943

The Promise

Everything we may rightly expect from God, all that we are permitted to pray for, is to be found in Jesus Christ. Everything that we might imagine a god can and should do has nothing to do with the God of Jesus Christ. Again and again we must immerse ourselves quietly for long periods of time in the life, teaching, ministry, suffering, and death of Jesus in order to recognize what it is that God promises and fulfills. It is certain that we may always live in the nearness and presence of God and that this life is an entirely new life for us, that there is no longer anything impossible for us, that no earthly power can touch us without God's will, and that danger and distress only drive us closer to God. It is certain that we may claim nothing and yet may ask for everything. It is certain that in suffering our joy is hidden, in dying our life is hidden. It is certain that in everything we stand in a community of faith that bears us up and sustains us. To all this God has spoken Yes and Amen in Jesus (2 Corinthians 1:20). This Yes and Amen is the firm ground on which we stand. Again and again in these turbulent times we let slip out of our sight why it is actually worthwhile to live. The truth of the matter, however, is that when the earth was counted worthy to have the man Jesus Christ dwell on it, when a person like Jesus has lived here, then and only then is there a meaning in our own life here. If Jesus had not lived, then despite all the other people that we know, respect, and love, our life would be meaningless. The unbiblical term "meaning" is of course a translation of what the Bible calls "promise."

It is difficult for me not to be able to help you now at all—except that every morning and evening, and while reading the Bible, and often at other times during the day, I think of you.

Dietrich Bonhoeffer to Eberhard Bethge,
Tegel prison, April 30, 1944

The Answer

It is always good to be reminded that the pastor can never please the proper "layperson." If I preach grace and faith alone, you ask, "Then what about the responsibilities of Christian living?" If I preach from the Sermon on the Mount, you ask, "What about real life?" If I give an interpretation of a truly real and sinful life of someone in the Bible (King David), then you ask, "What about the eternal truths, the abiding principles?" And from all this we should probably hear only one concern: how in this real world do I live a Christian life, and what are the ultimate authorities for the only one kind of life worth living?

To begin with, I will confess quite simply: I believe that the Bible alone is the answer to all our questions and that to receive an answer from it, we only need to ask with persistence and a little courage. One cannot *read* the Bible as we read other books. One must be ready to really ask questions. Only in this way does it open itself up to us. Only when we wait expectantly before it for the ultimate answer does it give it to us. The reason for this is simply that in the Bible it is God who speaks to us. And when it comes to God, one cannot just think things out for oneself; one must ask God. Only when we seek God does he answer. Of course, the Bible can *also* be read like any other book, for example, from the point of view of such disciplines as text criticism. Nothing whatsoever is to be said against such a reading. The only problem is, with these methods one can get only the surface meaning of the biblical text, not its essential message. Just as we do not grasp the word of someone we love by first analyzing it but just by accepting it and allowing it to echo within us for days simply as the word of this loved one, and as we then get to know the one who has spoken this word better and better the more we "ponder the word in our hearts" like Mary (Luke 2:19)—this is the way we should deal with the word of the Bible. Only when we once dare to read ourselves into the Bible as though it really is God who speaks to us here, the God who loves us and will not finally abandon us to our questions, only then will reading the Bible become a joy.

It is always the case that we can only seek that which we already know. If I do not really know what I am looking for, I'm not really seeking. Thus we must already know which God we are looking for before we can really seek him. If I do not know that, then I drift from place to place, and "seeking" becomes an end in itself, and finding is no longer the main thing. Thus I can only find when I know what or whom I am seeking. Now either I know this God whom I am seeking on my own, by my experiences and insights, from nature or history interpreted this way or that—and this means I know God by myself, from my own resources—or I know God by his revelation in his own word. Either I determine the place where I will find God, or I let God determine the place where he wants to be found. If I am the one who gets to decide where God will be found, then I will always find a God there, a God who some way or other is the kind of God I am looking for, a God I like, a God appropriate to my own nature and personality. But if God is the One who says where he will be found, then this will very likely be the place that at first does not at all fit my own nature and character, a place I probably will not like at all. This place is the cross of Jesus. And those who want to find God there must take their place under the cross, as demanded by the Sermon on the Mount. This does not at all correspond to our own nature; it is exactly contrary to it. But this is the message of the Bible, not only in the New Testament but also in the Old Testament (Isaiah 53!). In any case this was the understanding of both Jesus and Paul: in the cross of Jesus the Scripture, that is, the Old Testament, is fulfilled. Thus the whole Bible is permeated by the divine intention of being that word in which God wants to be found by us. No place that seems pleasant to us, or that at first even seems reasonable to us, but a place in every way strange to us, totally alien to us. Precisely there is the place God has chosen to meet us.

This is the way I now read the Bible. I ask of every passage, "What does God have to say to us here?" And I ask God what he wants to say. Thus we can no longer look for general, eternal truths, principles that correspond to our own "eternal" nature and as such can be made obvious. Rather, we seek the will of God, the One who is entirely strange and contrary to us, whose ways are not our ways and whose thoughts are not our thoughts, who conceals himself under the sign of the cross, the One in whom all our ways and thoughts have found their end. God is wholly other than so-called eternal truth. That is always an "eternal" we have thought out and wanted for ourselves. But God's word begins by pointing to the cross of Jesus, the place where all our ways and thoughts finally lead—including our "eternal truths"—namely, to death and standing before God in judgment.

From this point of departure can you then somehow understand that I will not surrender the Bible as this strange word of God; on the contrary, I will ask with all my powers what God is trying to say to us through it. Every other place outside the Bible has become too uncertain for me. I fear that there I will only bump into my own divine look-alike, a reflection of myself. Is it then also conceivable that I am now more prepared for a *sacrificium intellectus* (offering my intellect as a sacrifice [to God])—even in these things and only in these things, that is, in view of the God of truth. And who is there who would not actually offer his or her own *sacrificium intellectus* on some altar or other? This means confessing that one does not yet understand this or that passage in the Scripture, in the confidence that it also will be revealed one day as God's own word. I would rather do this than to go ahead and say at my own discretion, "This is divine, that is merely human"!

And I want to say something to you quite personally: since I have learned to read the Bible in this way—which has not been long at all—it becomes more wonderful to me each day. I read some every morning and evening, often also during the day, and every day I take one text that I keep for the whole week and try to immerse myself in it in order really to hear it. I know that without this I could no longer truly live. Even less would I be able to believe. Every day more and more riddles are resolved; we are still stuck too much on the surface of the text. When I was recently again in Hildesheim and saw some art from the Middle Ages, it became clear to me how people in those days understood the Bible much more than today. In their struggles our ancestors in the faith had nothing more than the Bible and did not want to have any more, and by it they became independent and firm in an authentic life of faith. And this is something that makes one think. I believe it would be quite superficial to respond that since then everything has become very different. Human beings have certainly remained the same, and so have their troubles. And the Bible answers them today no less than back then. It may be that this is a very basic matter. But you would not believe what a joy it is when one has found one's way back from barking up the wrong tree of so many theologians on these basic matters. And, I believe, in matters of faith we are always all in the same basic boat.

In a few days it will be Easter. I am very much looking forward to it. But do you think that any of us could and would want to believe these impossible things reported in the Gospels if they were not in the Bible? It is simply a matter of the word, as the truth of God, for which God himself is the guarantor. Resurrection is, after all, not a very reasonable concept in itself, not an "eternal truth." Of course, I mean it in the same sense the Bible means it—as resurrection from real death (not from "sleep") to real life, from being distant from God, from Godlessness itself, to new life in Christ with God. God said—and we know it from the Bible—"See, I am making all things new" (Revelation 21:5). This is what God made come true at Easter. Would not this message appear even more impossible, strange, bizarre than the whole story of King David, which is almost harmless by comparison?

The only thing left is the decision whether we are willing to trust the word of the Bible or not, whether we are willing to let ourselves be held by it, as by no other word in life or in death. And, I believe, we can find true joy and peace only when we have made this decision. . . .

Table of Sources

DB Eberhard Bethge. *Dietrich Bonhoeffer, Theologe—Christ—Zeitgenosse: Eine Biographie.* 7th rev. ed. Munich and Gütersloh: Chr. Kaiser and Gütersloher Verlagshaus, 2001.

DBW *Dietrich Bonhoeffer Werke.* Edited by Eberhard Bethge et al. 17 vols. Munich and Gütersloh: Chr. Kaiser and Gütersloher Verlagshaus, 1986–1999.

Vol. 1 (DBW 1): *Sanctorum Communio: Eine dogmatische Untersuchung zur Soziologie der Kirche.* Edited by Joachim von Soosten. 1986.

Vol. 2 (DBW 2): *Akt und Sein: Transzendentalphilosophie und Ontologie in der systematischen Theologie.* Edited by Hans-Richard Reuter. 1988. 2d ed., 2002.

Vol. 3 (DBW 3): *Schöpfung und Fall.* Edited by Martin Rüter and Ilse Tödt. 1989. 2d ed., 2002.

Vol. 4 (DBW 4): *Nachfolge.* Edited by Martin Kuske and Ilse Tödt. 1989. 3d ed., 2002.

Vol. 5 (DBW 5): *Gemeinsames Leben: Das Gebetbuch der Bibel.* Edited by Gerhard L. Müller and Albrecht Schönherr. 1987. 2d ed., 2002.

Vol. 6 (DBW 6): *Ethik.* Edited by Ilse Tödt et al. 1992. 2d ed., 1998.

Vol. 7 (DBW 7): *Fragmente aus Tegel.* Edited by Renate Bethge and Ilse Tödt. 1994.

Vol. 8 (DBW 8): *Widerstand und Ergebung.* Edited by Christian Gremmels et al. 1998.

Vol. 9 (DBW 9): *Jugend und Studium, 1918–1927.* Edited by Hans Pfeifer with Clifford Green and Carl-Jürgen Kaltenborn. 1986.

Vol. 10 (DBW 10): *Barcelona, Berlin, Amerika, 1928–1931.* Edited by Hans Christoph von Hase et al. 1991.

Vol. 11 (DBW 11): *Ökumene, Universität, Pfarramt, 1931–1932.* Edited by Eberhard Amelung and Christoph Strohm. 1994.

Vol. 12 (DBW 12): *Berlin, 1932–1933.* Edited by Carsten Nicolaisen and Ernst Albert Scharffenorth. 1997.
Vol. 13 (DBW 13): *London, 1933–1935.* Edited by Hans Goedeking, Martin Heimbucher, and Hans-Walter Schleicher. 1994.
Vol. 14 (DBW 14): *Illegale Theologenausbildung: Finkenwalde, 1935–1940.* Edited by Otto Dudzus et al. 1996.
Vol. 15 (DBW 15): *Illegale Theologenausbildung: Sammelvikariate, 1937–1940.* Edited by Dirk Schulz. 1998.
Vol. 16 (DBW 16): *Konspiration und Haft, 1940–1945.* Edited by Jørgen Glenthøj, Ulrich Kabitz, and Wolf Krötke. 1996.
Vol. 17 (DBW 17): *Register und Ergänzungen.* Edited by Herbert Anzinger et al. 1999.

(7) DB 51.
(9–10) DBW 14:112–13. Letter to Elisabeth Zinn, January 27, 1936.
(11) DBW 11:313.
(13–15 top) DBW 9:305–8. Works on theological orientation, 1925.
(15) DBW 12:314–15. Lectures on Christology, summer semester, 1933.
(17) DBW 11:353.
(19–21) DBW 3:25–26, 30, 34. Theological interpretation of Genesis 1–3, winter semester, 1932–1933.
(23–27) DBW 3:38–41. Theological interpretation of Genesis 1–3, winter semester, 1932–1933.
(29) DBW 8:50.
(31) DBW 10:350–51. Works from the Berlin period, 1930.
(33) DBW 11:403. Sermon on Matthew 24:6–14, February 1932.
(35–36) DBW 11:415–16. Meditation on John 8:31–32, 1932.
(37) DBW 6:141.
(39–50) DBW 11:426–35. Sermon, May 29, 1932.
(51) DBW 8:360.
(53–54) DBW 13:324–25. Sermon on 2 Corinthians 5:10, on the Day of Prayer and Repentance, November 19, 1933.
(55–57) DBW 13:351ff. Sermon on Psalm 98:1 at the Sunday cantata, April 29, 1934.
(59) DBW 8:72.
(61–66) DBW 5:38–43. Community Day, 1938.
(67) DBW 11:233.
(69–78) DBW 15:518–20, 523–29, 531–32. Meditations on Psalm 119, 1939–1940.
(79–81) DBW 16:23–24. Letter to Ruth Roberta Stahlberg, March 23, 1940.
(83) DBW 8:214–15.

(85–86)	DBW 16:488–89. Outline of a lecture on the theme "glory," 1940.
(87)	DBW 13:393.
(89–90)	DBW 16:495, 496, 497. Notes for a lecture, "Theology and Church," 1940.
(91)	DBW 16:325.
(93–94)	DBW 8:226–27. Letter to Eberhard Bethge on the second day of Advent, 1943.
(94–95)	DBW 8:499–501. Letter to Eberhard Bethge, June 27, 1944.
(95–96)	DBW 8:533–34. Letter to Eberhard Bethge, July 16, 1944.
(97)	DBW 8:548–49. Letter to Eberhard Bethge, July 28, 1944.
(97–99)	DBW 14:411ff. "Interpreting New Testament Texts for the Present." 1935.
(101)	DBW 8:69–70.
(103–104)	DBW 8:572–73. Letter to Eberhard Bethge, August 21, 1944.
(105)	DBW 8:402.
(107–12)	DBW 14:144–48. Letter to Rüdiger Schleicher, April 8, 1936.